JELL-O®
BRAND

KIDS'
COOKING
FUN

CRESCENT BOOKS

MESSAGE TO PARENTS

Children, like adults, feel positive about an experience if they are successful. JELL-O KIDS' COOKING FUN has been designed with children's cooking success in mind.

Each recipe has the ingredients and equipment highlighted in colored boxes to make it easy for the child to assemble everything he or she will need before beginning. The recipes are written in carefully illustrated steps so they are easy to follow. JELL-O MAN (the children's hero who saves their JELL-O gelatin and pudding from thieves) and his loyal dog WOBBLY help explain the steps of each recipe.

The first chapter of the book is called "The Real Easy Stuff," and it contains recipes for "Plain Gelatin" and "Plain Pudding." We encourage you to direct your child to those recipes first, as they are the building blocks for all the other recipes in the book. Once your child has mastered these, he or she can have fun making any of the other recipes.

Of course, you will want to make sure your child uses safe kitchen techniques. Spend time reading through and making sure your child understands "Rules of the Kitchen" on page 4. All recipes requiring adult supervision are clearly marked with appropriate symbols (see page 4 for explanation of these symbols) so that you will be able to clearly identify which recipes your child can make alone and which ones will require your help.

So tie on your aprons, review the "Rules of the Kitchen" with your child and have fun!

Copyright © 1991 Kraft General Foods, Inc.
All rights reserved.

ANGEL FLAKE, BAKER'S, COOL WHIP, JELL-O, JELL-O MAN, JIGGLERS, KRAFT and WOBBLY are trademarks of Kraft General Foods, Inc., Glenview, IL 60025.

UNO® is a registered trademark of International Games, Inc.

Pictured on front cover (*left to right*): Funny Face Desserts (*page 14*); Ice Cream Shop Pies - Pistachio Chocolate Bar Pie and Rocky Road Pie (*page 94*); Gelatin Pizza (*page 46*).

Pictured on back cover (*clockwise from top left*): JIGGLERS Birthday Dessert (*page 68*); Funny Face Desserts (*page 14*); Cookies & Cream Pudding Pie (*page 90*); Funny Face Desserts (*page 14*).

Library of Congress Catalog Card Number: 91-61024

ISBN: 0-517-059061

This edition published by
Crescent Books
Distributed by Outlet Book Company, Inc.
A Random House Company
225 Park Avenue South
New York, New York 10003

14

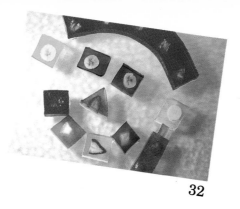
32

50

TABLE OF CONTENTS

56

68

84

RULES OF THE KITCHEN

1. Wash your hands with soap and water before you begin.

2. Read the **whole** recipe carefully before starting. If you don't understand any part, ask an adult to help you. Read "Cooking Tips," "Equipment" and "Cooking Words To Know" (pages 5-8) so you will know the meanings of all the words in the recipe.

3. Collect all the ingredients and equipment you need for the recipe before you start to cook.

4. Do one step of the recipe at a time. Do not skip steps.

5. Watch for symbols. Read and learn what the symbols mean (see below). When you see one of these symbols in the recipe, ask an adult to help you.

6. Measure carefully, using the correct equipment.

7. Use the size of pan called for in the recipe.

8. Follow the times given in the recipe. If a recipe says shake for 45 seconds, be sure you shake for at least 45 seconds.

9. Clean up when you are finished!

10. Share your tasty creations with family and friends.

SYMBOLS

Boiling water is used in the recipe. **Always have an adult help you** when you are using boiling water.

A microwave is used in the recipe. **Have an adult help you** select a microwavable bowl. Be careful when taking the bowl out of the microwave. Use pot holders because the bowl could be hot.

An oven is used in the recipe. **Have an adult help you** remove hot pans from the oven. **Always use pot holders.** Be sure to turn the oven off when you are finished.

A stove is used in the recipe. **Have an adult help you** set the right temperature. Use pot holders to handle hot pans. Be sure to turn the stove off when you are finished.

A sharp knife is used in the recipe. **Have an adult help you** cut and chop. Put the knife in a safe place when you are finished using it. Be sure to carry the knife point down!

The recipe may be a little difficult. **Have an adult help you** to make sure you understand how to make the recipe.

COOKING TIPS

Have an adult help you!

BOILING WATER

Boiling water on the stove

Boil water in a tea kettle. Pour the boiling water **carefully** into a measuring cup. Always put the tea kettle back on the stove.

Boiling water in the microwave

Pour water into a **microwavable** measuring cup. Microwave until water boils. Remove cup by handle **very carefully!** The cup could be very hot!

Remember, when you make JELL-O Gelatin, pour the boiling water **over** the gelatin. (Do **not** pour the gelatin **into** the boiling water.)

HOW TO MEASURE

When using a measuring cup, hold it at eye level to be sure that you have measured correctly.

Use a set of metal or plastic measuring spoons. Choose the right size spoon. When the recipe calls for a teaspoon or tablespoon, be sure to use measuring spoons, not the spoons you use for eating.

USING A SHAKER

1. Any 1-quart plastic container with a tight lid can be a shaker. After putting the ingredients into the shaker, put the lid on the shaker **very tightly.**

2. Put one hand on the top of the shaker and the other hand on the bottom of the shaker. Hold on very tightly. Shake hard for the amount of time given in the recipe.

EQUIPMENT

Be sure to use the right equipment if you want to be a good cook.

Yeah, yeah, yeah, yeah!

"Read your JELL-O boxes carefully."

"Check package size."

"Make sure you use *Instant*."

MEASURING EQUIPMENT

measuring spoons   measuring cups

BOWLS

small mixing bowl   medium mixing bowl   large mixing bowl

CONTAINERS

1-quart shaker with a tight lid (any plastic container with a tight lid will do) (4 cups = 1 quart)

PANS, ETC.

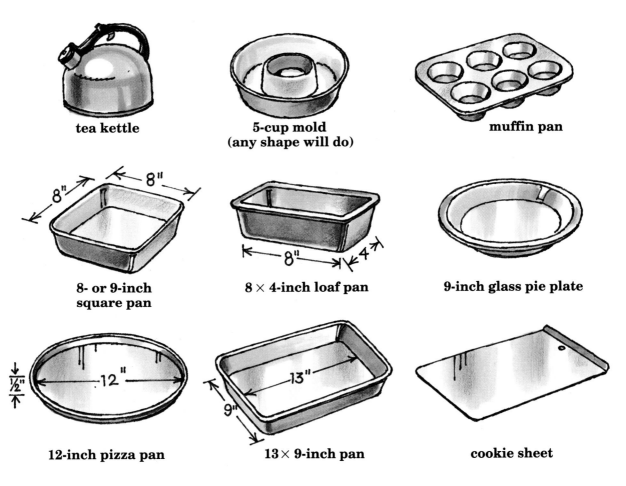

tea kettle

5-cup mold
(any shape will do)

muffin pan

8- or 9-inch
square pan

8 × 4-inch loaf pan

9-inch glass pie plate

12-inch pizza pan

13 × 9-inch pan

cookie sheet

UTENSILS AND TOOLS

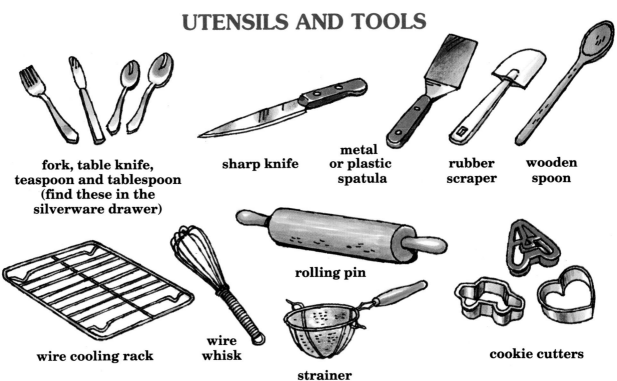

fork, table knife,
teaspoon and tablespoon
(find these in the
silverware drawer)

sharp knife

metal
or plastic
spatula

rubber
scraper

wooden
spoon

wire cooling rack

wire
whisk

rolling pin

strainer

cookie cutters

COOKING WORDS TO KNOW

BEAT – to stir hard

BLEND – to mix thoroughly

BOILING – when bubbles are popping in hot water

CHILL – to put into the refrigerator to cool

CHILL UNTIL SLIGHTLY THICKENED – when the mixture is thick like catsup

CHILL UNTIL THICKENED – when you pull a spoon through the mixture, it leaves a track

CHILL UNTIL SET – when you touch the mixture, it sticks to your finger

CHILL UNTIL FIRM – when you touch the mixture, it will wiggle

CHOP – to cut into small pieces

CRUMBLE – to break into crumbs

CRUSH – to break into very small bits using a tool such as a rolling pin

DISSOLVE GELATIN – to stir boiling water and gelatin until all the crystals disappear

STIR – to mix together with a large spoon or rubber scraper

THAW – to become unfrozen and soft

WEDGE – a piece shaped like a triangle

The Real Easy Stuff

Start here! Learn how to make easy, delicious "Plain Gelatin" and "Plain Pudding." After you've made them, you'll be enough of a JELL-O chef to make "Funny Face Desserts," "Buried Treasures" or "Milk Madness!"

FUNNY FACE DESSERTS
(recipe on page 14)

PLAIN GELATIN

INGREDIENTS	EQUIPMENT
1 package (4-serving size) JELL-O Gelatin, any flavor 1 cup boiling water 1 cup cold water	Medium mixing bowl Measuring cups Rubber scraper or large spoon 4 dessert dishes

1 **POUR** gelatin into bowl.

2 **ADD** 1 cup boiling water to gelatin.

3 **STIR** with rubber scraper until gelatin is completely dissolved, about 2 minutes.

4 **ADD** 1 cup cold water. Stir. Using measuring cup, scoop gelatin into dessert dishes.

5 **PUT** dishes into refrigerator to chill until firm, about 3 hours.

Makes 4 servings

PLAIN PUDDING

<table>
<tr><td>

INGREDIENTS

2 cups cold milk
1 package (4-serving size)
   JELL-O Instant Pudding,
   any flavor

</td><td>

EQUIPMENT

Measuring cup
1-quart shaker with a tight lid
4 dessert dishes

</td></tr>
</table>

1 POUR 2 cups of cold milk into shaker.

2 ADD pudding mix. Put lid on shaker very tightly.

3 SHAKE very hard for at least 45 seconds. (Be sure to hold top and bottom of shaker tightly.)

4 **OPEN** shaker. Pour pudding into dessert dishes. Pudding will thicken quickly and be ready to eat in 5 minutes. If you do not want to eat the pudding right away, put dishes into refrigerator to chill until serving time.

Makes 4 servings

FUNNY FACE DESSERTS

INGREDIENTS	EQUIPMENT
2 cups cold milk **1 package (4-serving size)** **JELL-O Instant Pudding,** **any flavor** **Decorations, such as: fruit,** **candies, nuts, chocolate** **chips, peanut butter chips,** **miniature marshmallows,** **coconut**	**Measuring cup** **1-quart shaker with a tight lid** **4 dessert dishes**

1 **POUR** 2 cups of cold milk into shaker. Add pudding mix. Put lid on shaker very tightly. Shake very hard for at least 45 seconds. (Be sure to hold top and bottom of shaker tightly.)

2 **OPEN** shaker. Pour pudding into dessert dishes. Let pudding stand for 5 minutes. Make faces on the pudding with decorations. Eat immediately, if you wish, or put dishes into refrigerator to chill until serving time.

OR

MAKE faces on JELL-O Gelatin. Make Plain Gelatin (see page 10). Pour gelatin into 4 dessert dishes. After gelatin is firm, make the faces.

Makes 4 servings

BURIED TREASURES

INGREDIENTS

"Treasures," such as:
   broken cookies, miniature
   marshmallows, peanut
   butter, fruit, chocolate
   chips, nuts
2 cups cold milk
1 package (4-serving size)
   JELL-O Instant Pudding,
   any flavor

EQUIPMENT

Measuring spoons
4 dessert dishes
Measuring cup
1-quart shaker with a tight lid
Large spoon

1 **CHOOSE** 4 different "treasures" to "bury." You will need about 2 tablespoons of each treasure. Put a treasure on the bottom of each dessert dish. You may put more than one treasure in each dish, if you wish!

2 **POUR** 2 cups of cold milk into shaker. Add pudding mix. Put lid on shaker very tightly. Shake very hard for at least 45 seconds. (Be sure to hold top and bottom of shaker tightly.)

3 **OPEN** shaker. Gently spoon or pour pudding from shaker over the treasures. Pudding will thicken quickly and be ready to eat in 5 minutes. If you do not want to eat the pudding right away, put dishes into refrigerator to chill until serving time.

Makes 4 servings

BREAKFAST MAGIC

INGREDIENTS	EQUIPMENT
1 package (4-serving size) JELL-O Gelatin, any flavor Cold cereal with milk OR Any sliced fruit OR Ready-to-eat waffles Butter	Spoon or sprinkler (empty, clean salt shaker will do) Table knife

Sprinkle some dry gelatin over cereal and watch the magic color appear!

OR

Sprinkle some dry gelatin over your favorite fruit.

OR

Prepare waffles, following package directions. Butter waffles with table knife while they are still warm. Immediately sprinkle some dry gelatin over waffles. The more you sprinkle on, the brighter the color.

If you have leftover gelatin, fold up package to use another time.

MILK MADNESS

<table>
<tr><td>

INGREDIENTS

1 cup cold milk
2 tablespoons JELL-O
    Gelatin, any flavor *except*
    lemon

</td><td>

EQUIPMENT

Measuring cup
1-quart shaker with a tight lid
Measuring spoons
Drinking glass

</td></tr>
</table>

1 **POUR** 1 cup of cold milk into shaker.

2 **SPRINKLE** 2 tablespoons of gelatin over milk. Put lid on shaker very tightly.

3 **SHAKE** very hard for at least 1 minute. (Be sure to hold top and bottom of shaker tightly.) Open shaker. Pour into glass. Drink right away.

Makes 1 serving

If you have leftover gelatin, fold up package to use another time.

EASY PUDDING MILKSHAKE

INGREDIENTS

1 cup cold milk

2 tablespoons JELL-O Instant Pudding, any flavor

1 scoop (½ cup) ice cream, any flavor, softened

EQUIPMENT

Measuring cup

1-quart shaker with a tight lid

Measuring spoons

Ice cream scoop or ½ cup measure

Drinking glass

1 POUR 1 cup of cold milk into shaker. Add 2 tablespoons of pudding mix and the ice cream. Put lid on shaker very tightly.

2 SHAKE very hard for at least 1 minute. (Be sure to hold top and bottom of shaker tightly.)

3 OPEN shaker. Pour into glass. Drink right away.

Makes 1 serving

If you have leftover pudding mix, fold up package to use another time.

FLUFFY PUDDING FROSTING

<table>
<tr><th>INGREDIENTS</th><th>EQUIPMENT</th></tr>
<tr><td>

1 cup cold milk

1 package (4-serving size) JELL-O Instant Pudding, any flavor

3½ cups (8-ounce container) COOL WHIP Whipped Topping, thawed

24 plain cupcakes

Candy decorations, if you wish

</td><td>

Measuring cup

Large mixing bowl

Wire whisk

Rubber scraper or large spoon

Teaspoon

</td></tr>
</table>

1 **POUR** 1 cup of cold milk into bowl. Add pudding mix.

2 **BEAT** with wire whisk until well blended, about 2 minutes.

3 **STIR** whipped topping into pudding **very gently** with rubber scraper until mixture is all the same color.

4 **PLACE** about a spoonful of frosting on each cupcake. Spread frosting around top of cupcake with the back of the teaspoon. Sprinkle with candy decorations, if you wish. Put cupcakes into refrigerator to chill until serving time. Store any leftover cupcakes in refrigerator.

Frosts 24 cupcakes

FAVORITE FUN TOPPINGS

Top off your JELL-O Pudding and JELL-O Gelatin recipes with all kinds of fun toppings. These are some of JELL-O MAN's and WOBBLY's favorites. You may want to add some of your own.

chocolate chips	gum drops	nuts
jelly beans	miniature marshmallows	red hot candies
string licorice	nonpareils	gummy bears
butterscotch chips	candy corn	jellied fruit slices
peanut butter chips	plain or toasted coconut	multi-colored milk chocolate candies

JIGGLERS Mania

*What's more fun than making and eating JIGGLERS?
Going crazy over "JIGGLERS Surprises," "JIGGLERS
Pineapple Snacks" and more!*

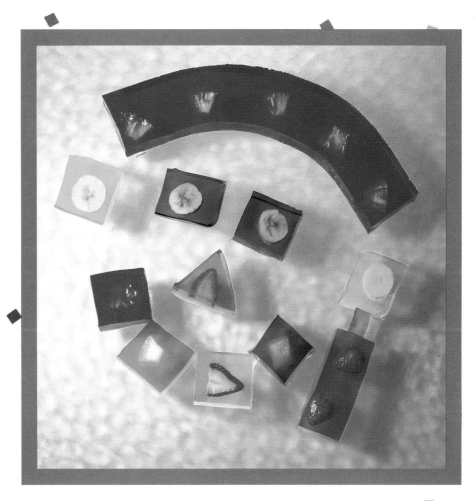

JIGGLERS "SURPRISES"
(recipe on page 32)

JIGGLERS

Gelatin Snacks

INGREDIENTS

4 packages (4-serving size each) OR 2 packages (8-serving size each) JELL-O Gelatin, any flavor

2½ cups boiling water

EQUIPMENT

Medium mixing bowl
Measuring cup
Rubber scraper or large spoon
13 x 9-inch pan
Small cookie cutters or table knife

1 POUR gelatin into bowl. Add 2½ cups boiling water to gelatin. Stir with rubber scraper until gelatin is completely dissolved, about 2 minutes.

2 POUR into 13 x 9-inch pan. Put pan into refrigerator to chill until firm, about 3 hours.

3 TAKE pan out of refrigerator. Put about 1 inch of warm water in sink. Dip **just bottom** of pan into warm water for 15 seconds.

4 **USE** cookie cutters to cut gelatin into any shapes you wish. (If you do not have cookie cutters, cut gelatin into squares with a table knife.)

5 **LIFT** shapes out of pan with your fingers.

Makes about 24 small shapes

Use any leftover pieces to make "Scrap Happy" (see page 40).

JIGGLERS, CREAMY-STYLE

INGREDIENTS	EQUIPMENT
4 packages (4-serving size each) OR 2 packages (8-serving size each) JELL-O Gelatin, any flavor 2½ cups boiling water 1 cup cold milk 1 package (4-serving size) JELL-O Instant Pudding, Vanilla Flavor	Medium mixing bowl Measuring cup Rubber scraper or large spoon 1-quart shaker with a tight lid Wire whisk 13 x 9-inch pan Small cookie cutters or table knife

1 POUR gelatin into bowl. Add 2½ cups boiling water to gelatin. Stir with rubber scraper until gelatin is completely dissolved, about 2 minutes. Cool to room temperature, about 30 minutes.

2 POUR 1 cup of cold milk into shaker. Add pudding mix. Put lid on shaker very tightly. Shake very hard for at least 1 minute. (Be sure to hold top and bottom of shaker tightly.)

3 OPEN shaker. Pour pudding quickly into gelatin. Stir with wire whisk until mixture is all the same color. Pour into 13 x 9-inch pan. Put pan into refrigerator to chill until firm, about 3 hours.

4 **TAKE** pan out of refrigerator. Put about 1 inch of warm water in sink. Dip **just bottom** of pan into warm water for 15 seconds.

5 **USE** cookie cutters to cut gelatin into any shapes you wish. (If you do not have cookie cutters, cut gelatin into squares with a table knife.) Lift shapes out of pan with your fingers.

Makes about 24 small shapes

Use any leftover pieces to make "Scrap Happy" (see page 40).

JIGGLERS "SURPRISES"

<table>
<tr><th>INGREDIENTS</th><th>EQUIPMENT</th></tr>
</table>

INGREDIENTS

- **4 packages (4-serving size each) OR 2 packages (8-serving size each) JELL-O Gelatin, any flavor**
- **2½ cups boiling water**
- **36 "surprises," such as: banana slices, strawberry halves, canned pineapple chunks**

EQUIPMENT

Medium mixing bowl
Measuring cup
Rubber scraper or large spoon
13 x 9-inch pan
Table knife

1 POUR gelatin into bowl. Add 2½ cups boiling water to gelatin. Stir with rubber scraper until gelatin is completely dissolved, about 2 minutes. Pour into 13 x 9-inch pan.

2 LET pan of gelatin stand on counter for 30 minutes. Gelatin will become thickened.

3 ARRANGE "surprises" in rows in thickened gelatin so that, when cut, each square will have a surprise. Put pan into refrigerator to chill until firm, about 3 hours. Take pan out of refrigerator.

4 **PUT** about 1 inch of warm water in sink. Dip **just bottom** of pan into warm water for 15 seconds. With table knife, cut gelatin into shapes, making sure you have a piece of fruit in each shape. Lift shapes out of pan with your fingers.

Makes about 36 small shapes

Use any leftover pieces to make "Scrap Happy" (see page 40).

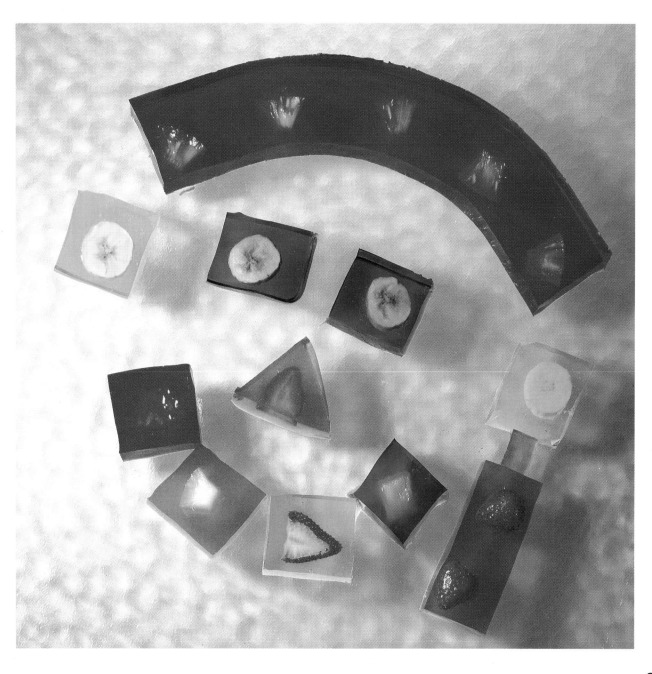

JIGGLERS ALPHABET

<table>
<tr><td>

INGREDIENTS

4 packages (4-serving size each) OR 2 packages (8-serving size each) JELL-O Gelatin, any flavor

2½ cups boiling water

</td><td>

EQUIPMENT

Medium mixing bowl
Measuring cup
Rubber scraper or large spoon
13 x 9-inch pan
Paper and pencil
Alphabet cutters
Tray or large plate

</td></tr>
</table>

1 **POUR** gelatin into bowl. Add 2½ cups boiling water to gelatin. Stir with rubber scraper until gelatin is completely dissolved, about 2 minutes.

2 **POUR** into 13 x 9-inch pan. Put pan into refrigerator to chill until firm, about 3 hours. Take pan out of refrigerator. Put about 1 inch of warm water in sink. Dip **just bottom** of pan into warm water for 15 seconds.

3 **WRITE** down on a piece of paper the words you wish to use. Then, use alphabet cutters to cut out each JIGGLERS letter you need. Lift letters out of pan with your fingers. Arrange letters into your words on a tray.

Makes about 25 (2-inch) letters

Use any leftover pieces to make "Scrap Happy" (see page 40).

34

Can you make a sentence from these words? (Answer is on page 40.)

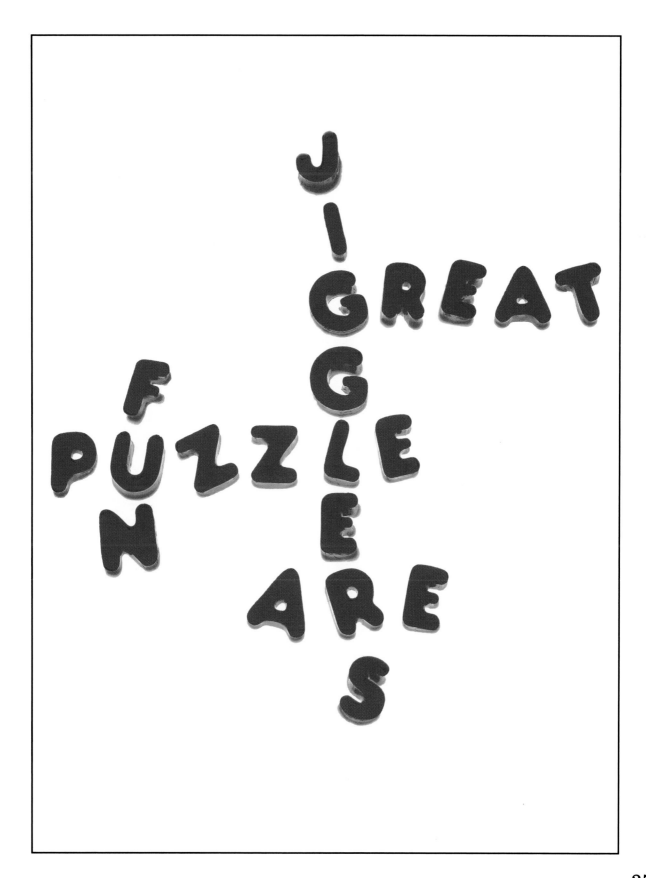

JIGGLERS SAILBOAT

INGREDIENTS

4 packages (4-serving size each) OR 2 packages (8-serving size each) JELL-O Gelatin, Orange Flavor

2½ cups boiling water

4 packages (4-serving size each) OR 2 packages (8-serving size each) JELL-O Gelatin, Lime Flavor

2½ cups boiling water
COOL WHIP Whipped Topping, thawed, if you wish

EQUIPMENT

2 medium mixing bowls
Measuring cup
Rubber scraper or large spoon
2 (13 x 9-inch) pans
Table knife
Metal or plastic spatula
Paper and pencil to make paper pattern, if you wish
Scissors
Large tray
Zipper-style plastic sandwich bag

1 **POUR** orange gelatin into bowl. Add 2½ cups boiling water to gelatin. Stir with rubber scraper until gelatin is completely dissolved, about 2 minutes. Pour into one of the 13 x 9-inch pans.

2 **PREPARE** lime gelatin in same way as orange gelatin. Put both pans into refrigerator to chill until firm, about 3 hours. After both pans of gelatin are firm, take them out of refrigerator. Put about 1 inch of warm water in sink. Dip **just bottom** of each pan into warm water for 15 seconds.

3 CUT out pieces with a table knife for your sailboat using the two colors of gelatin to make different parts for your sailboat. (You may wish to make shapes from paper first and use them as a guide.) Lift sailboat pieces out of pans with your fingers or spatula. Put sailboat together on large tray.

4 SPOON whipped topping into zipper-style plastic sandwich bag. Squeeze extra air out of bag; close top tightly. Snip a **tiny** corner off bottom of bag with scissors. Squeeze bag gently to decorate sailboat. Decorate with other cutouts, if you wish.

Makes 1 large sailboat

Use any leftover pieces to make "Scrap Happy" (see page 40).

JIGGLERS
PINEAPPLE SNACKS

<table>
<tr><td>

INGREDIENTS

4 packages (4-serving size each) OR 2 packages (8-serving size each) JELL-O Gelatin, any flavor

2 cups boiling water

1 can (8 ounces) crushed pineapple with juice, undrained

</td><td>

EQUIPMENT

Medium mixing bowl
Measuring cup
Rubber scraper or large spoon
13 x 9-inch pan
Small cookie cutters or table knife

</td></tr>
</table>

1 **POUR** gelatin into bowl. Add 2 cups boiling water to gelatin. Stir with rubber scraper until gelatin is completely dissolved, about 2 minutes. Add crushed pineapple with juice. Stir. Pour into 13 x 9-inch pan.

2 **PUT** pan into refrigerator to chill until firm, about 3 hours. Take pan out of refrigerator. Put about 1 inch of warm water in sink. Dip **just bottom** of pan into warm water for 15 seconds.

3 **USE** cookie cutters to cut gelatin into shapes. (If you do not have cookie cutters, cut gelatin into shapes with a table knife.) Lift shapes out of pan with your fingers or table knife.

Makes about 36 small shapes

Use any leftover pieces to make "Scrap Happy" (see page 40).

SCRAP HAPPY

After you have made JELL-O JIGGLERS, you can use the leftovers to make a delicious snack—"Scrap Happy."

Make a "dish" by spreading thawed COOL WHIP Whipped Topping over the bottom and up the sides of a small bowl. Tear the scraps from your JIGGLERS into little pieces with your fingers. Then fill each bowl with the JIGGLERS scraps. Put bowls into refrigerator to chill until serving time.

Puzzle answer: JIGGLERS ARE GREAT PUZZLE FUN.

Rainy Day Fun

Being stuck in the house on a rainy day doesn't have to be boring. Whip up a few "Dirt Cups," a "Gelatin Pizza" or some "Colorful Candy Popcorn Balls" and have your own little party.

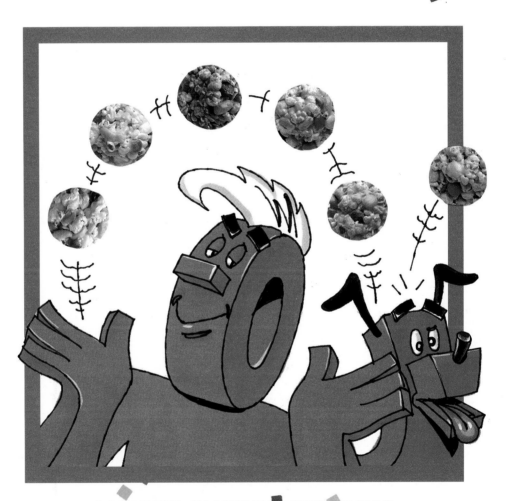

COLORFUL CANDY POPCORN BALLS
(recipe on page 50)

DIRT CUPS

INGREDIENTS

- 2 cups cold milk
- 1 package (4-serving size) JELL-O Instant Pudding, Chocolate Flavor
- 3½ cups (8-ounce container) COOL WHIP Whipped Topping, thawed
- 1 package (16 ounces) chocolate sandwich cookies, crushed, divided

EQUIPMENT

Measuring cup
Medium mixing bowl
Wire whisk
Rubber scraper or large spoon
Measuring spoons
8 to 10 paper or plastic cups (8 ounces each)
Baseball decorations, if you wish

1 **POUR** 2 cups of cold milk into bowl. Add pudding mix. Beat with wire whisk until well blended, about 2 minutes. Let pudding stand 5 minutes.

2 **STIR** whipped topping and ½ of the crushed cookies into pudding **very gently** with rubber scraper until mixture is all the same color. Place about 1 tablespoon of the remaining crushed cookies into bottom of each paper or plastic cup.

3 **FILL** cups about ¾ full with pudding mixture. Top each cup with the rest of the crushed cookies. Put cups into refrigerator to chill until set, about 1 hour. Add baseball decorations, if you wish.

Makes 8 to 10 Dirt Cups

Make your favorite baseball pennants out of paper and toothpicks. You can make a baseball diamond out of licorice and candies. If you have small plastic baseball players, use them too!

FRIENDSHIP COOKIES

INGREDIENTS

1 package (15 ounces) golden sugar cookie mix (plus ingredients to prepare mix)

1 package (4-serving size) JELL-O Gelatin, any flavor

Flour

Tubes of decorating gel or icing

Assorted candies

EQUIPMENT

Medium mixing bowl
Wooden spoon
Rolling pin
Cookie cutters
Cookie sheet
Plastic straw
Metal or plastic spatula
Wire cooling racks
Ribbon or string

1 **PREHEAT** oven to 375°. Prepare cookie mix in bowl following package directions, but **do not add water** to the mix. Stir gelatin into cookie dough with spoon until well blended. Sprinkle flour lightly on counter. Roll out dough with rolling pin so it is ¼ inch thick.

2 **USE** cookie cutters to cut out any shapes you wish. Place cookies about 1 inch apart on ungreased cookie sheet. Poke a hole at top of each cookie with plastic straw. Bake at 375° for 6 to 8 minutes or until lightly browned.

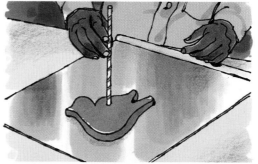

3 **REMOVE** cookies from cookie sheet with spatula. Place on wire racks; cool completely. Decorate each cookie as you wish, using tubes of decorating gel and assorted candies. Put a ribbon through hole in each cookie. Tie ribbons so you can hang cookies.

Makes about 30 cookies

GELATIN PIZZA

<table>
<tr><td>

INGREDIENTS

4 packages (4-serving size each) OR 2 packages (8-serving size each) JELL-O Gelatin, any flavor
2½ cups boiling water
   No-stick cooking spray
1 cup thawed COOL WHIP Whipped Topping
2 cups cut-up fruit

</td><td>

EQUIPMENT

Medium mixing bowl
Measuring cup
Rubber scraper or large spoon
12-inch pizza pan with ½-inch sides
Table knife or pizza cutter
Metal spatula

</td></tr>
</table>

1 **POUR** gelatin into bowl. Add 2½ cups boiling water to gelatin. Stir with rubber scraper until gelatin is completely dissolved, about 2 minutes. Spray inside of pizza pan with no-stick cooking spray. Pour gelatin mixture into pizza pan. Put pan into refrigerator to chill until firm, about 3 hours.

2 **TAKE** pan out of refrigerator when ready to serve. Put about 1 inch of warm water in sink. Carefully dip **just bottom** of pan into warm water for 15 seconds. Spread whipped topping over gelatin with rubber scraper, leaving about 1 inch of space around outside edge of gelatin for pizza "crust."

3 **TOP** pizza with fruit, arranging fruit in whatever design you like. Cut pizza into wedges with table knife. Lift pizza wedges from pan with spatula.

Makes 10 to 12 servings

CHOCOLATE PUDDING COOKIES

<table>
<tr><td>

INGREDIENTS

1 **package (4-serving size) JELL-O Instant Pudding, Chocolate Flavor**
1 **cup buttermilk baking mix**
¼ **cup oil**
1 **egg**
Peanut butter chips or other assorted candies

</td><td>

EQUIPMENT

Measuring cups
Large mixing bowl
Wooden spoon
Tablespoon
Cookie sheet
Metal or plastic spatula
Wire cooling racks

</td></tr>
</table>

1 PREHEAT oven to 350°. Put pudding mix and baking mix in bowl. Mix together with wooden spoon. Add oil and egg. Mix together until mixture forms a ball.

2 TAKE a small spoonful of dough and shape it into a ½-inch ball. Place ball on ungreased cookie sheet. Shape rest of dough into ½-inch balls. Place balls about 2 inches apart on ungreased cookie sheet.

3 PRESS your thumb into middle of each ball to make a thumbprint. Put peanut butter chips or candies in thumbprint. Bake at 350° for 5 to 8 minutes or until lightly browned. Remove cookies from cookie sheet with spatula. Place on wire racks; cool.

Makes about 36 cookies

COLORFUL CANDY POPCORN BALLS

INGREDIENTS	EQUIPMENT
12 cups popped popcorn	Measuring cups
1 cup peanuts	Huge bowl or very large pot
¾ cup multi-colored milk chocolate candies	Wooden spoon
¼ cup (½ stick) margarine	Large microwavable bowl
1 bag (10½ ounces) KRAFT Miniature Marshmallows	Pot holders
1 package (4-serving size) JELL-O Gelatin, any flavor	Waxed paper
Margarine for greasing your hands	

1 **POUR** popcorn into huge bowl. Add peanuts and milk chocolate candies. Mix together with spoon.

2 **PUT** margarine and marshmallows in large **microwavable** bowl. Microwave on HIGH 1½ to 2 minutes or until marshmallows are puffed. Using pot holders, take bowl out of microwave. (**Careful! Bowl will be hot.**) Mix together with spoon.

3 **ADD** gelatin to marshmallow mixture. Stir with spoon until mixture is all the same color.

4 **POUR** marshmallow mixture over popcorn mixture in huge bowl. Quickly stir with spoon until marshmallow mixture evenly covers popcorn mixture. Let mixture cool slightly. **Grease your hands well** with some margarine. Shape mixture into balls with your hands. Place balls on waxed paper until completely cool.

Makes about 24 popcorn balls

51

MORE FUN WITH DIRT CUPS

There are many ways you can have fun with "Dirt Cups." Just make "Dirt Cups" (see page 42). Then plant a garden! Add silk or plastic flowers, candy worms, frogs or bugs. Or—make a racetrack with little cars! Or—place a tiny doll under an umbrella. Make a special "Dirt Cup" for each member of your family!

Sleepover Surprises

Invite your friends to a sleepover party. When they arrive, put on your favorite music, make some "Pudding Pile-Ons" or "Brownie Pudding Pizza" and party! Continue the food fun in the morning with "Pink Banana Pancakes."

BROWNIE PUDDING PIZZA
(recipe on page 56)

PUDDING PILE-ONS

INGREDIENTS

1 package (17 ounces) refrigerated sugar cookie dough

Flour

1¼ cups cold milk

1 package (4-serving size) JELL-O Instant Pudding, any flavor

1 cup thawed COOL WHIP Whipped Topping

Toppings, such as: chocolate chips, peanut butter chips, coconut, miniature marshmallows, nuts, multi-colored milk chocolate candies

EQUIPMENT

Table knife
Cookie sheet
Metal or plastic spatula
Wire cooling racks
Measuring cups
Small mixing bowl
Wire whisk
Rubber scraper or large spoon
Tablespoon

1 PREHEAT oven to 350°. Cut cookie dough with table knife into ½-inch slices. Sprinkle flour lightly on counter. Pat each slice to make a **large** circle, about 4 to 5 inches across. Place circles 2 inches apart on ungreased cookie sheet.

2 BAKE at 350° for 10 to 12 minutes or until lightly browned. Remove cookies from cookie sheet with spatula. Place on wire racks; cool.

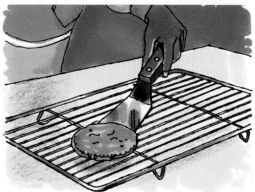

3 POUR 1¼ cups of cold milk into bowl. Add pudding mix. Beat with wire whisk until well blended, about 2 minutes. Let pudding stand 5 minutes. Stir whipped topping into pudding **very gently** with rubber scraper until mixture is all the same color

4 IF you do not want to prepare and eat the desserts right away, put pudding mixture into refrigerator to chill until serving time. Just before serving, spread about 3 spoonfuls of pudding mixture over each cookie with back of spoon. Decorate with toppings.

Makes 10 to 12 Pudding Pile-Ons

BROWNIE PUDDING PIZZA

INGREDIENTS	EQUIPMENT
1 package (10½ ounces) microwave brownie mix (plus ingredients to prepare mix)	Medium mixing bowl
1¼ cups cold milk	9-inch microwavable pie plate
1 package (4-serving size) JELL-O Instant Pudding, any flavor	Pot holders
1 cup thawed COOL WHIP Whipped Topping	Measuring cups
2 cups cut-up fruit	Small mixing bowl
	Wire whisk
	Rubber scraper or large spoon
	Tablespoon
	Sharp knife

1 **PREPARE** brownie mix in medium bowl, following package directions. Pour mixture into 9-inch **microwavable** pie plate. Microwave, following package directions for 9-inch square pan. Using pot holders, take pie plate out of microwave. **(Careful! Plate will be hot.)** Cool.

2 **POUR** 1¼ cups of cold milk into small bowl. Add pudding mix. Beat with wire whisk until well blended, about 2 minutes. Let pudding stand 5 minutes.

3 **STIR** whipped topping into pudding **very gently** with rubber scraper until mixture is all the same color. If you do not want to prepare and eat pizza right away, put pudding mixture into refrigerator to chill until serving time. Just before serving, spoon pudding mixture over brownies, spreading with back of spoon to cover evenly.

4 **CUT** into wedges. Top each wedge with fruit, arranging fruit in whatever design you like.

Makes 8 servings

FRUIT TACOS

INGREDIENTS

1½ cups cold milk

1 package (4-serving size) JELL-O Instant Pudding, any flavor

1¾ cups (4-ounce container) COOL WHIP Whipped Topping, thawed

8 taco shells

2 cups cut-up fruit

½ cup BAKER'S ANGEL FLAKE Coconut

Chocolate syrup

EQUIPMENT

Measuring cups
Medium mixing bowl
Wire whisk
Rubber scraper or large spoon
Tablespoon

1 **POUR** 1½ cups of cold milk into bowl. Add pudding mix. Beat with wire whisk until well blended, about 2 minutes. Let pudding stand 5 minutes.

2 **STIR** whipped topping into pudding **very gently** with rubber scraper until mixture is all the same color. If you do not want to prepare and eat tacos right away, put pudding mixture into refrigerator to chill until serving time.

3 **JUST** before serving, spoon an equal amount of pudding mixture into each taco shell. Top with fruit and coconut. Pour a little chocolate syrup over filling.

Makes 8 Fruit Tacos

SHOCKING PINK DIP

INGREDIENTS	EQUIPMENT
1 **container (8 ounces) soft cream cheese** 1 **package (4-serving size) JELL-O Gelatin, any red flavor** ¼ **cup milk** **Fruit for dipping**	**Small mixing bowl** **Wooden spoon** **Measuring cup** **Wire whisk** **Serving bowl** **Large plate**

1 PUT cream cheese in small bowl.

2 ADD gelatin and milk to cream cheese. Beat with wire whisk until well blended and smooth. Put mixture into serving bowl. Put bowl into refrigerator to chill until serving time.

3 TAKE bowl out of refrigerator. Let dip stand at room temperature to soften slightly, if necessary (about 15 minutes). Place bowl on large plate. Arrange fruit on plate around serving bowl.

Makes about 1½ cups of dip

CHOCO-NUTTY DIP

INGREDIENTS	EQUIPMENT
½ cup creamy peanut butter 2½ cups cold milk 1 package (4-serving size) JELL-O Instant Pudding, Chocolate Flavor ¼ cup peanuts, if you wish Dippers, such as: marshmallows, graham crackers, pretzels, vanilla wafers	Measuring cups Small mixing bowl Wooden spoon Wire whisk Serving bowl Large plate

1 **PUT** peanut butter in small bowl. Stir peanut butter with spoon until smooth. Add 2½ cups of cold milk, a little at a time. Each time you add some milk, stir mixture again until smooth.

2 **ADD** pudding mix. Beat with wire whisk until well blended, about 2 minutes. Put mixture in serving bowl. Put bowl into refrigerator to chill until serving time.

3 **TAKE** bowl out of refrigerator. Sprinkle top of dip with peanuts, if you wish. Place serving bowl on large plate. Arrange dippers on plate around serving bowl.

Makes 3 cups of dip

PINK BANANA PANCAKES

INGREDIENTS	EQUIPMENT
1½ cups prepared pancake batter (Use pancake mix recipe for 12 to 16 pancakes.) 1 package (4-serving size) JELL-O Gelatin, any red flavor ½ cup chopped bananas	Medium mixing bowl Tablespoon Large skillet or griddle Metal or plastic spatula

1 **ADD** gelatin to prepared pancake batter in bowl.

2 **MIX** gelatin and pancake batter together with spoon until mixture is all the same color.

3 **GENTLY** stir in bananas. Cook pancakes, following package directions.

Makes 12 to 16 pancakes

MORE PANCAKE FUN

Hold a pancake contest! Make different shapes and decorate the pancakes. Give a prize to the person who makes the funniest-shaped pancake.

Perfect Parties

Holidays and birthdays are times for extra special desserts. Celebrate with "Easy Easter Basket Cake," "Jack-O'-Lantern Pie" and "JIGGLERS Birthday Dessert."

JIGGLERS BIRTHDAY DESSERT
(recipe on page 68)

JIGGLERS
BIRTHDAY DESSERT

INGREDIENTS

1 package (4-serving size) JELL-O Gelatin, Strawberry or any other red flavor

1¼ cups boiling water

4 packages (4-serving size each) OR 2 packages (8-serving size each) JELL-O Gelatin, Lemon Flavor

4 cups boiling water

1 pint vanilla ice cream, softened

EQUIPMENT

2 medium mixing bowls

Measuring cup

Rubber scraper or large spoon

8- or 9-inch square pan

Wooden spoon

13 x 9-inch pan or any shallow 2-quart baking dish

Alphabet cutters

1 POUR strawberry gelatin into bowl. Add 1¼ cups boiling water to gelatin. Stir with rubber scraper until gelatin is completely dissolved, about 2 minutes. Pour into 8-inch square pan. Put pan into refrigerator to chill until firm, about 3 hours.

2 POUR lemon gelatin into the other bowl. Add 4 cups boiling water to gelatin. Stir with rubber scraper until gelatin is completely dissolved, about 2 minutes.

3 **ADD** ice cream to lemon gelatin. Stir with rubber scraper until ice cream is melted and mixture is smooth. Pour into 13 x 9-inch pan. Put pan into refrigerator to chill until firm, about 3 hours.

4 **TAKE** both pans out of refrigerator. Put about 1 inch of warm water in sink. Dip **just bottom** of strawberry gelatin pan into warm water for 15 seconds. Use alphabet cutters to cut out letters for "Happy Birthday." Lift letters out of pan with your fingers. Place letters on lemon gelatin.

Makes 12 servings

Use any leftover pieces to make "Scrap Happy" (see page 40).

JIGGLERS VALENTINES

INGREDIENTS	EQUIPMENT
4 packages (4-serving size each) OR 2 packages (8-serving size each) JELL-O Gelatin, any red flavor 2½ cups boiling water COOL WHIP Whipped Topping, thawed Sprinkles for decoration, if you wish	Medium mixing bowl Measuring cup Rubber scraper or large spoon 13 x 9-inch pan Small heart-shaped cookie cutters Tablespoon Zipper-style plastic sandwich bag Scissors

1 **POUR** gelatin into bowl. Add 2½ cups boiling water to gelatin. Stir with rubber scraper until gelatin is completely dissolved, about 2 minutes. Pour into 13 x 9-inch pan. Put pan into refrigerator to chill until firm, about 3 hours. Take pan out of refrigerator.

2 **PUT** about 1 inch of warm water in sink. Dip **just bottom** of pan into warm water for 15 seconds. Use cookie cutters to cut gelatin into hearts. Lift hearts out of pan with your fingers.

3 **SPOON** some whipped topping into zipper-style plastic sandwich bag. Squeeze extra air out of bag; close top tightly. Snip a **tiny** corner off bottom of bag with scissors.

4 SQUEEZE bag gently to make designs or to write on hearts. Add sprinkles for decoration, if you wish. You can use leftover scraps to make more decorations to put on your hearts or to make "Scrap Happy" (see page 40).

Makes about 36 small hearts

EASY EASTER BASKET CAKE

INGREDIENTS	EQUIPMENT
1 **package (4-serving size) JELL-O Gelatin, Lime Flavor** 1 **cup boiling water** ¾ **cup cold water** 1 **pound cake loaf (about 12 ounces)** 1¾ **cups (4-ounce container) COOL WHIP Whipped Topping, thawed** **Licorice stick** **Jelly beans**	**Medium mixing bowl** **Measuring cup** **Rubber scraper or large spoon** **8- or 9-inch square pan** **Fork** **Large tray** **Table knife or spreader**

1 POUR gelatin into bowl. Add 1 cup boiling water to gelatin. Stir with rubber scraper until gelatin is completely dissolved, about 2 minutes. Add ¾ cup cold water. Stir. Pour into 8-inch square pan. Put pan into refrigerator to chill until firm, about 3 hours.

2 TAKE pan out of refrigerator. Break gelatin into small flakes with fork. (Pull fork across gelatin firmly, pressing all the way to bottom of pan.) Set flakes aside.

3 REMOVE cake from wrapper and place on large tray. Frost top and sides of cake with whipped topping using table knife. Carefully place flaked gelatin on top of cake.

4 CURVE licorice stick and poke into the cake for basket handle. Put cake into refrigerator to chill until serving time. Decorate with jelly beans just before serving.

Makes 12 servings

To make bunny: Take 1 large marshmallow; use thawed COOL WHIP Whipped Topping to stick bits of jelly beans onto rounded side of marshmallow to form eyes. Stick on a small piece of red string licorice for mouth. Put 3 miniature marshmallows on each of 2 toothpicks for ears. Attach them to head. Attach large marshmallow for body with additional toothpick.

FLAG POKE CAKE

INGREDIENTS

Margarine

Flour

1 package (2-layer size) white cake mix (plus ingredients to prepare mix)

1 package (4-serving size) JELL-O Gelatin, any red flavor

1 cup boiling water

½ cup cold water

3½ cups (8-ounce container) COOL WHIP Whipped Topping, thawed

1 pint strawberries, sliced

1 cup blueberries

1 cup KRAFT Miniature Marshmallows

EQUIPMENT

13 x 9-inch pan

Large fork

Medium mixing bowl

Measuring cups

Rubber scraper or large spoon

Large tray or cutting board

Table knife

1 **GREASE** 13 x 9-inch pan with margarine. Dust pan with flour. Prepare cake mix, following package directions. Pour batter into pan and bake following package directions for 13 x 9-inch pan. Cool cake in pan for 15 minutes. Make holes in cake every ½ inch, using large fork.

2 **POUR** gelatin into bowl. Add 1 cup boiling water to gelatin. Stir with rubber scraper until gelatin is completely dissolved, about 2 minutes. Add ½ cup cold water. Stir. With measuring cup, scoop gelatin out of bowl and pour it over cake. Put cake into refrigerator to chill, about 3 to 4 hours.

3 **TAKE** pan out of refrigerator. Put about 1 inch of warm water in sink. Dip **just bottom** of pan into warm water for 10 seconds. Put large tray upside down on top of cake. Holding tightly, turn tray and pan over, so pan is on top and tray is on bottom. (Have an adult help you.) Take pan off.

4 **FROST** top and sides of cake with whipped topping, using table knife. Arrange strawberries, blueberries and marshmallows on cake so it looks like a flag. Put cake into refrigerator to chill until serving time.

Makes 12 to 15 servings

Store any leftover cake in refrigerator.

JACK-O'-LANTERN PIE

INGREDIENTS	EQUIPMENT

INGREDIENTS

1 package (4-serving size) JELL-O Gelatin, Orange Flavor

1 cup boiling water

1 pint vanilla ice cream, softened

1 9-inch chocolate crumb crust

  Candy corn

  Black licorice, cut into 1-inch pieces

  COOL WHIP Whipped Topping, thawed, for decoration, if you wish

EQUIPMENT

Medium mixing bowl

Measuring cup

Rubber scraper or large spoon

Wooden spoon

Zipper-style plastic sandwich bag

Scissors

1 POUR gelatin into bowl. Add 1 cup boiling water to gelatin. Stir with rubber scraper until gelatin is completely dissolved, about 2 minutes.

2 ADD ice cream to gelatin. Stir with rubber scraper until ice cream is melted and mixture is smooth.

3 **PUT** bowl into refrigerator to chill until slightly thickened, about 10 minutes. Take bowl out of refrigerator. Pour mixture into crust. Put pie into refrigerator to chill until firm, about 2 hours. Take pie out of refrigerator. Make a jack-o'-lantern face on pie with candy corn and licorice.

4 **DECORATE** with whipped topping, if you wish. Spoon whipped topping into zipper-style plastic sandwich bag. Squeeze extra air out of bag; close top tightly. Snip a small corner off bottom of bag with scissors. Squeeze bag gently to make design.

Makes 8 servings

JIGGLERS CANDY CANE

<table>
<tr><td>

INGREDIENTS

4 packages (4-serving size each) OR 2 packages (8-serving size each) JELL-O Gelatin, any red flavor

4 cups boiling water

1 cup thawed COOL WHIP Whipped Topping
   Colored sprinkles

</td><td>

EQUIPMENT

Medium mixing bowl
Measuring cup
Rubber scraper or large spoon
13 x 9-inch pan
Table knife
Paper and pencil to make
 paper pattern, if you wish
Scissors
Large tray
Zipper-style plastic sandwich
 bag

</td></tr>
</table>

1 **POUR** gelatin into bowl. Add 4 cups boiling water to gelatin. Stir with rubber scraper until gelatin is completely dissolved, about 2 minutes. Pour into 13 x 9-inch pan. Put pan into refrigerator to chill until firm, about 3 hours.

2 **TAKE** pan out of refrigerator. Put about 1 inch of warm water in sink. Dip **just bottom** of pan into warm water for 15 seconds.

3 **CUT** out 1 large candy cane shape from gelatin with table knife. (You may wish to make shape from paper first, and use it as a guide.) Take away extra gelatin so only cane is in pan. Lift out cane and place it on large tray. (Have an adult help you.)

78

4 **SPOON** whipped topping into zipper-style plastic sandwich bag. Squeeze extra air out of bag; close top tightly. Snip a small corner off bottom of bag with scissors. Squeeze bag gently to make stripes on candy cane. Add sprinkles on stripes.

Makes 12 servings

Cut leftover gelatin with cookie cutters to make other holiday shapes. Try decorating them, too.

MORE POKE CAKE IDEAS

Poke cakes are pretty to see and fun to eat. You can make lots of different kinds following the directions on page 74. Try orange gelatin for a Halloween poke cake. Use lime gelatin for a St. Patrick's Day cake. For a Valentine's Day cake, use red gelatin. Frost your cake with whipped topping. Add decorations to match the special day.

Family Dinners.

You will be the star of the family when you make one of these super recipes for dinner. Whether you choose "Muffin Pan Snacks," "Strawberry-Banana Salad" or "Pudding Poke Cake," your whole family will be impressed.

STRAWBERRY-BANANA SALAD
(recipe on page 84)

MUFFIN PAN SNACKS

<table>
<tr><td>

INGREDIENTS

1 package (4-serving size)
   JELL-O Gelatin, Orange,
   Lemon or Lime Flavor
1 cup boiling water
1 cup cold water
1½ cups diced vegetables, such
   as: fresh carrots, celery or
   cucumber; or frozen mixed
   vegetables, thawed,
   drained

</td><td>

EQUIPMENT

Medium mixing bowl
Measuring cup
Rubber scraper or large spoon
Muffin pan

</td></tr>
</table>

1 POUR gelatin into bowl. Add 1 cup boiling water to gelatin. Stir with rubber scraper until gelatin is completely dissolved, about 2 minutes.

2 ADD 1 cup cold water. Using measuring cup, scoop gelatin from bowl into 6 muffin pan cups.

3 PUT pan into refrigerator to chill until gelatin is thickened, about 45 minutes. Take pan out of refrigerator. Add vegetables to each cup; stir gently. Put pan into refrigerator to chill until firm, about 2 hours.

4 **PUT** about 1 inch of warm water in sink. Dip **just bottom** of pan into warm water for 5 seconds. Dip your fingers in warm water. Gently pull gelatin from edge of pan with wet fingers. Lift snacks out of pan with your fingers.

Makes 6 snacks

STRAWBERRY-BANANA SALAD

INGREDIENTS	EQUIPMENT
2 packages (4-serving size each) JELL-O Gelatin, Strawberry or Strawberry-Banana Flavor 1½ cups boiling water 1 cup cold water Ice cubes 2 medium bananas, sliced No-stick cooking spray Mixed fresh fruit, such as: strawberry halves, banana slices, grapes (about 2 cups)	Large mixing bowl 2-cup measuring cup Rubber scraper or large spoon 4-cup mold Serving plate

1 POUR gelatin into bowl. Add 1½ cups boiling water to gelatin. Stir with rubber scraper until gelatin is completely dissolved, about 2 minutes.

2 POUR 1 cup cold water into 2-cup measuring cup. Add enough ice cubes to make 1¾ cups in all. Add the ice cubes and water to gelatin mixture. Stir until slightly thickened. Remove any unmelted ice.

3 **LET** gelatin stand until thickened, 5 to 10 minutes. Gently stir in sliced bananas. Spray inside of mold with no-stick cooking spray. Pour gelatin mixture into mold. Put mold into refrigerator to chill until firm, about 2 hours. Take mold out of refrigerator.

4 **PUT** about 4 inches of warm water in sink. Dip mold into warm water **just to top** of mold for 10 seconds. Dip your fingers in warm water. Gently pull gelatin from edge of mold with wet fingers.

5 **PUT** plate upside down on top of mold. Holding tightly, turn mold and plate over so mold is on top and plate is on bottom. (Have an adult help you.) Shake gently to loosen gelatin. Take mold off. Arrange fresh fruit inside or around mold, as you wish.

Makes 8 servings

TACO SALAD MOLD

INGREDIENTS

3 packages (4-serving size each) JELL-O Gelatin, Lemon Flavor

1 teaspoon salt

2½ cups boiling water

1 jar (16 ounces) taco sauce, medium flavor

3 tablespoons vinegar

1 teaspoon chili powder

1 package (10 ounces) frozen sweet corn, thawed, drained

No-stick cooking spray

Shredded lettuce, sour cream and tortilla chips, if you wish

EQUIPMENT

Medium mixing bowl

Measuring spoons

Measuring cup

Rubber scraper or large spoon

5-cup mold

Serving plate or tray

1 POUR gelatin into bowl. Add salt. Add 2½ cups boiling water to gelatin and salt. Stir with rubber scraper until gelatin is completely dissolved, about 2 minutes.

2 ADD taco sauce, vinegar and chili powder to gelatin mixture. Stir. Put bowl into refrigerator to chill until slightly thickened, about 1 hour. Take bowl out of refrigerator. Stir in corn.

If you do not have a mold, you can make the salad in a bowl.

3 **SPRAY** inside of mold with no-stick cooking spray. Pour gelatin mixture into mold. Put mold into refrigerator to chill until firm, about 4 hours.

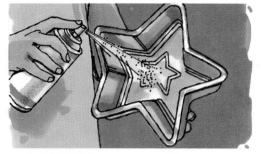

4 **TAKE** mold out of refrigerator. Put about 4 inches of warm water into sink. Dip mold in warm water **just to top** of mold for 10 seconds. Dip your fingers in warm water. Gently pull gelatin from edge of mold with wet fingers.

5 **PUT** plate upside down on top of mold. Holding tightly, turn mold and plate over so mold is on top and plate is on bottom. (Have an adult help you.) Shake gently to loosen gelatin. Take mold off. Serve with shredded lettuce, sour cream and tortilla chips, if you wish.

Makes 10 to 12 servings

PUDDING POKE CAKE

INGREDIENTS

1 **pound cake loaf** (about 12 ounces)
1½ **cups cold milk**
1 **package** (4-serving size) **JELL-O Instant Pudding, Chocolate Flavor**
Candy decorations, if you wish

EQUIPMENT

Serving plate
Wooden spoon
Measuring cups
1-quart shaker with a tight lid
Table knife

1 REMOVE cake from wrapper and place it on plate. Poke 25 to 30 holes into top of cake with handle of wooden spoon.

2 POUR 1½ cups of cold milk into shaker. Add pudding mix. Put lid on shaker very tightly. Shake very hard for at least 45 seconds. (Be sure to hold top and bottom of shaker tightly.)

3 POUR about ¼ of the pudding mixture quickly over holes in cake. Tap cake lightly on counter so pudding will go down holes. Pour about ⅓ of the rest of the pudding over holes. Tap cake again.

4 LET rest of pudding stand 2 minutes to thicken. Frost sides and top of cake with remaining pudding using table knife. Put cake into refrigerator to chill until serving time. Sprinkle with candy decorations, if you wish.

Makes 8 to 10 servings

COOKIES & CREAM PUDDING PIE

INGREDIENTS	EQUIPMENT
26 chocolate sandwich cookies **1½** cups cold milk **1** cup (½ pint) vanilla ice cream, softened **1** package (4-serving size) JELL-O Instant Pudding, Chocolate Flavor **COOL WHIP** Whipped Topping, thawed, for decoration, if you wish	9-inch pie plate Measuring cup Medium mixing bowl Wire whisk Zipper-style plastic sandwich bag Scissors

1 PLACE cookies on bottom and sides of pie plate. Cookies should cover plate evenly.

2 POUR 1½ cups of cold milk into bowl. Add ice cream. Beat with wire whisk until well blended. Add pudding mix. Beat with wire whisk until well blended, about 2 minutes. Let pudding stand for 3 minutes.

3 **POUR** pudding into cookie-lined pie plate. Put pie into refrigerator to chill until set, about 3 hours. To decorate, spoon whipped topping into zipper-style plastic sandwich bag. Squeeze extra air out of bag; close top tightly. Snip a small corner off bottom of bag with scissors. Squeeze bag gently to make design. Chill until serving time.

Makes 8 servings

TOFFEE BAR CRUNCH PIE

INGREDIENTS

⅓ cup butterscotch sauce

1 packaged graham cracker crust

1½ cups cold half-and-half or milk

1 package (4-serving size) JELL-O Instant Pudding, Vanilla Flavor

3½ cups (8-ounce container) COOL WHIP Whipped Topping, thawed

1 cup chopped chocolate-covered English toffee bars (about 6 bars)

Additional toffee bars, chopped, if you wish

EQUIPMENT

Measuring cups
Tablespoon
Large mixing bowl
Wire whisk
Rubber scraper

1 POUR butterscotch sauce onto bottom of pie crust. Spread gently with back of spoon to cover evenly.

2 POUR 1½ cups of cold half-and-half into bowl. Add pudding mix. Beat with wire whisk until well blended, about 2 minutes. Let pudding stand until slightly thickened, about 5 minutes.

3 **STIR** whipped topping and chopped toffee bars into pudding **very gently** with rubber scraper until mixture is all the same color. Spoon mixture into crust.

4 **PUT** pie in freezer for 6 hours or overnight. Remove pie from freezer. Let pie stand at room temperature about 10 minutes before serving. Decorate with chopped toffee bars, if you wish.

Makes 8 servings

Store any leftover pie in the freezer.

ICE CREAM SHOP PIES

Now that you are a super cook, invent your very own pie. Use the "Toffee Bar Crunch Pie" on page 92 as your basic recipe. Change the crust, the sauce, the pudding flavor and the candies and you have a new pie! Here are 2 changes to the "Toffee Bar Crunch Pie" to get you started. Now make up your own! Fill in the chart so you have a record of your recipe.

	Toffee Bar Crunch Pie	Pistachio Chocolate Bar Pie	Rocky Road Pie	*My Pie*
Sauce	Butterscotch	Chocolate	Chocolate	
Crust	Graham Cracker	Chocolate Crumb	Chocolate Crumb	
JELL-O Instant Pudding Flavor	Vanilla	Pistachio	Chocolate	
Candy Add-Ins	1 cup chopped chocolate-covered English toffee bars	1 cup chopped chocolate candy bars	½ cup chocolate chips and ½ cup KRAFT Miniature Marshmallows	

Index